FERGUSON
CAREER BIOGRAPHIES

SALLY
RIDE

Astronaut

Joanne Mattern

Ferguson
An imprint of Infobase Publishing

Sally Ride: Astronaut

Ferguson
An imprint of Infobase Publishing
132 West 31st Street
New York NY 10001

Library of Congress Cataloging-in-Publication Data

Mattern, Joanne, 1963–
   Sally Ride : astronaut / Joanne Mattern.
       p. cm.
   Includes index.
   ISBN 0-8160-5892-X (hc : alk. paper)
   1. Ride, Sally—Juvenile literature. 2. Women astronauts—United States—Biography—Juvenile literature. 3. Astronauts—United States—Biography—Juvenile literature.
I. Title.
   TL789.85.R53M38 2006
   629.45′0092—dc22   2005011185

Ferguson books are available at special discounts when purchased in bulk quantities for businesses, associations, institutions, or sales promotions. Please call our Special Sales Department in New York at (212) 967-8800 or (800) 322-8755.

You can find Ferguson on the World Wide Web at http://www.fergpubco.com

Text design by David Strelecky

Pages 83–113 adapted from Ferguson's *Encyclopedia of Careers and Vocational Guidance, Thirteenth Edition*

Printed in the United States of America

MP Hermitage 10 9 8 7 6 5 4 3 2 1

This book is printed on acid-free paper.

CONTENTS

1

FIRST U.S. WOMAN IN SPACE

Early in the morning of June 18, 1983, the space shuttle *Challenger* stood on the launch pad at the Kennedy Space Center in Cape Canaveral, Florida. There were five astronauts on board the shuttle, waiting for liftoff. For the first time in U.S. history, one of those astronauts was a woman. Sally Ride was about to become the first American woman to travel into space.

As the shuttle's engines ignited, a tremendous roar filled the spacecraft. Then, liftoff! The shuttle rose from the launch pad in a blast of fire, smoke, and steam. Inside the craft, the five crew members heard the noise of the rockets. The force of the launch pinned them back into their seats. Then the rockets and fuel tank broke away from the rocket and fell back to Earth. About 44 minutes after launch, the shuttle was in orbit 200 miles above the Earth, and Sally and the other crew members were in space.

Sally Ride made history on that June morning. She had trained for the space mission for a year, but had been getting ready for a career as an astronaut for much longer. Her lifelong love of science had made her a pioneer, both for scientists and for women.

Sally was overwhelmed when she first blasted into space and wasn't sure what to expect. As she later told an interviewer, "I didn't know whether I was going to be exhilarated or terrified. Actually, what washed over me and what blanked out my mind was a feeling of complete helplessness, like there was so much power that there was nothing I could do to change what was happening." Despite her initial nervousness, Sally soon became very comfortable in space and later said that it was the best experience of her life.

Sally Ride is best remembered for that shuttle flight. However, her career has continued to take interesting twists and turns in the years since that sunny June morning. As well as flying on two shuttle flights, Sally also served as one of the investigators of the *Challenger* shuttle disaster and became part of NASA's management. Then she left NASA and focused her energies on teaching and writing books about space for children. She now works to encourage young women to pursue careers in

Sally Ride, shown here aboard the space shuttle Challenger *in 1983, is the first U.S. woman in space.* (Bettmann/Corbis)

science. To accomplish this goal, Sally has started a national club to link girls with the scientific community and give them opportunities to take part in science camps and research projects. Sally also spends many days each year traveling around the United States and speaking to audiences about the future of women in science.

"The message is that there are, in fact, lots and lots of girls out there who can go out and do great things in science, engineering, and technology," Sally once told an audience, "but they need the support." Sally Ride aims to give them that support. Her career has shown that anyone can forge a path as a scientist and researcher—and that this path can lead well beyond our planet.

2

AN ACTIVE CHILDHOOD

Sally Kristen Ride was born in Encino, California, on May 26, 1951. Her parents were Dale and Joyce Ride. Sally was Dale and Joyce's first child. Two years later, the family welcomed Sally's sister, Karen. Sally could not say Karen's name when she was little, so she called her new sister "Bear." The nickname stuck, and Karen was known as Bear throughout her childhood.

Dale Ride was a political science teacher at Santa Monica College. Sally's mother had also been a teacher, but she stayed home to care for Sally and Karen. Although she did not work full time outside of the home, Joyce did teach English to foreign students. She also volunteered at the Encino Presbyterian Church and at a nearby women's prison.

The Ride home was casual and loving. Dale and Joyce were easygoing and did not have a lot of daily rules. A friend of Sally's said that no one was required to sit at the table for dinner in the Ride home, and family members could eat what they liked, as long as it was healthy.

A Love of Reading

Education was very important in the Ride home. The house was full of books, and both parents frequently read to the children. By the time she was five years old, Sally knew how to read. Growing up, her favorite books were science fiction and mysteries. She especially enjoyed books featuring Nancy Drew and James Bond, two popular characters who had many adventures. Superman was also one of Sally's favorite characters.

Sally also loved to read about sports. She could often be found curled up in a chair with the daily newspaper, studying the sports pages and memorizing statistics about her favorite baseball players.

Star Athlete

Sally was not just interested in reading about sports: She loved to play them too. She was one of the best athletes in the neighborhood. Sally joined the neighborhood children in games of soccer, baseball, and football. Her favorite sport was softball. Sally was so good at softball that she was the only girl in the neighborhood who was welcome to play on the boys' team. In fact, the boys often picked

Sally first for their team! At that time, many people did not think girls could be as good at sports as boys. Sally's experience showed her that girls and boys could compete and play together. Skill and experience were what mattered, not whether a person was male or female.

Joyce and Dale Ride encouraged Sally and Karen to take part in any activity that interested them. They respected their children's interests and encouraged them to try new things. The only rule was that the girls had to study hard and do their best. "Dale and I simply forgot to tell them that there were things they couldn't do," Joyce Ride later admitted.

The family soon learned that Sally could not be forced to do anything she didn't want to do. One year, Joyce tried to get Sally to take piano lessons. It soon became clear that Sally was not interested in piano, so her mother gave up. "If Sally was interested in a subject, she'd give it all her attention," Joyce later said about her daughter. "If she wasn't interested, she didn't give it her attention. She sets her own goals and competes with herself."

A Trip to Europe

The Rides always felt it was important to expose their children to other cultures. Dale met many foreign exchange students and professors from other countries at his teaching job. He often invited these visitors home for dinner. Sally and Karen loved these visits and eagerly listened to stories of faraway lands.

When Sally was nine and Karen was seven years old, their parents decided it was time for the girls to experience other countries firsthand. They planned to spend a year traveling around Europe. Dale took a leave of absence from his job, and the family set off on their trip.

The journey to Europe became one of the most important and exciting experiences of Sally's childhood. She and her sister traveled through many different countries. They visited castles, mountains, cities, and farms. Every day was a new adventure.

Although Sally and Karen did not attend school during their year in Europe, they kept learning. Dale and Joyce tutored the girls. They based their lessons on their daily experiences in Europe. The girls studied the governments and history of each country they visited. They learned about new languages and studied the cultures and customs of many different places. Sally's mother later said that Sally and Karen had learned as much from traveling as they would have in school.

When the Rides arrived back in Encino, Sally realized just how much she had learned on the trip. She was now far ahead of her classmates. Because of this, she skipped a grade and was allowed to join a class of older children.

Sally did well in school, where her favorite subjects were science and math. Despite her abilities, she did not stand out. She was quiet and a little bit shy, and did her work without making much of a fuss. One of her teachers at Portola Junior High School later said Sally was not "remarkable in any way—she was just a good student."

The only problem Sally had with school was that she was sometimes bored by the lessons. If a subject did not interest her, it was hard for Sally to pay attention. After one teacher described Sally as "a clock watcher," Sally responded that both the teacher and the class were so dull, she couldn't help but be anxious for the class to be over!

Tennis, Anyone?

Sally continued to be interested in sports. Soon after they came back from Europe, Joyce and Dale began playing tennis. Sally thought the game looked fun and wanted to learn how to play too. Sally spent hours in her driveway hitting a tennis ball against the garage door. Soon she had such good aim that she could hit any spot she wanted.

Sally loved to play tennis, and she was very good at it. She was not afraid to challenge anyone to a match. She even played against adults, and she often won. Sally's parents realized how talented and determined their daughter was to succeed at tennis. They arranged for her to have lessons from Alice Marble, who was a four-time women's national tennis champion.

By the time she was in her early teens, Sally was ranked nationally as an amateur tennis player. She spent weekends traveling all over the United States to compete in tournaments, and at one point was ranked number 18 out of all the junior tennis players in the country. Sally's family wondered if she would become a professional tennis player when she got older.

A New School

Sally's tennis skills drew the attention of the faculty at Westlake School for Girls. Westlake was a small, private high school in Los Angeles. The headmaster of the school wanted Sally on their tennis team and was also impressed by her academic abilities. He offered Sally a scholarship to attend Westlake. She accepted.

Sally enjoyed her new school. Along with playing tennis, she excelled in academic subjects. Then, during her junior year, she took a class that changed her life.

Sally enrolled in a class called physiology, which is the study of the function and workings of living things. Sally was fascinated by the class. She became good friends with the teacher, Dr. Elizabeth Mommaerts. Dr. Mommaerts saw how excited Sally was about science and worked with her to pursue her interests. She often gave Sally extra experiments to work on outside of class and gave her books to read. Sally later described Dr. Mommaerts as "intelligent, clear-thinking, and extremely logical," all of which were qualities Sally admired.

Dr. Mommaerts taught Sally about the scientific method, which is a system used to investigate scientific problems and come up with new ideas about how and why things happen. The scientific method includes several steps, such as observation, creating a hypothesis or theory, performing experiments, gathering data, and drawing conclusions. This careful approach to learning appealed to Sally because it was so logical. She enjoyed conducting experiments and making observations and loved the challenge of testing new theories and ideas.

The Lure of Space

The 1950s and 1960s were an exciting time in the American scientific community. On October 4, 1957, the Soviet Union sent the first satellite into space. This satellite, called *Sputnik I*, was just a 184-pound metal ball (about two feet in diameter) that orbited the Earth. It was a humble beginning to the space program, but it stunned the United States.

At the time, the United States and the Soviet Union were bitter rivals, especially in the area of technology. The United States was ashamed to admit that it did not have rockets powerful enough to launch a satellite into space, and that the Soviet Union had done something beyond the U.S. program's ability. The U.S. government also worried that the Soviets might use their rocket power to attack the United States. One U.S. Senator called _Sputnik I_'s launch, "a week of shame and danger." An editorial cartoon in the _Detroit Free Press_ showed the Russian satellite knocking Uncle Sam's star-spangled hat right off his head.

The launch of _Sputnik I_ pushed the United States' space program into high gear. Over the next six months, Russia sent up two more satellites, and the United States sent up three. The space program had become a competition, and the news media were filled with stories about the "space race."

Soviet cosmonaut Yuri Gagarin was the first man to orbit Earth. (Associated Press)

As it had with satellite launches, the Soviet Union also won the race to put a human being into orbit. On April 12, 1961, Soviet cosmonaut (the Russian word for astronaut) Yuri Gagarin soared into space aboard a spaceship called

Vostok I. Gagarin, a major and pilot in the Soviet army, orbited the Earth one time in his tiny craft and then parachuted safely back to Earth. Once again, the Soviets rejoiced at their accomplishment, while the United States could only watch in dismay.

The United States was already working to send its own astronaut into space. A number of test pilots had been recruited into the space program, which was operating under a government agency called the National Aeronautics and Space Administration, or NASA for short. On May 5, 1961, one of these pilots, Alan Shepard, made a 15-minute flight above the Earth in a spacecraft called *Freedom 7.* Shepard did not orbit the Earth, but his journey was a big step forward for the U.S. space program.

While the space program continued to work on getting someone into orbit, President John F. Kennedy had a greater goal in mind. On May 25, 1961, President Kennedy made a speech to Congress. In it, he said, "I believe that this nation should commit itself to achieving the goal, before this decade is out, of landing a man on the moon and returning him safely to Earth. No single space project in this period will be more impressive to mankind, or more important for the long-range exploration of space."

On February 20, 1962, the United States finally achieved its goal of sending a man into orbit. John Glenn, another

President John F. Kennedy did much to advance the U.S. space program. In this speech to Congress in 1961, he urged the nation to commit to landing a man on the moon during the 1960s. (NASA Headquarters—Greatest Images of NASA)

test pilot, rocketed into orbit aboard the spacecraft _Friendship 7_. Although there were some scary moments when automatic controls aboard the craft malfunctioned, Glenn was able to complete three orbits and return safely to Earth. He was greeted as a national hero and received a presidential welcome and a ticker-tape parade through the streets of New York City.

This quest for space captured the attention of many Americans—including Sally Ride. Along with her family, she watched America's exploration of space on television. She cheered triumphs, such as Shepard's and Glenn's flights. She also worried when things went wrong, as they did on July 21, 1961. On that day, astronaut Gus Grissom almost drowned after his craft, *Liberty Bell 7*, splashed down into the Atlantic Ocean. An explosive charge meant to blast the bolts off the escape hatch detonated too early, and Grissom had to escape quickly before his craft sank.

Astronaut John Glenn inspects the Friendship 7 (NASA Headquarters—Greatest Images of NASA)

Apollo

The space program moved forward throughout the 1960s. Although NASA continued to send astronauts into space on brief flights with projects known as Mercury and Gemini, the focus was on the greater goal of landing on the moon. Although the Mercury and Gemini flights did not travel to the moon, these flights helped NASA design better spacecraft, understand what went on during space travel, and invent procedures that would later be used in the moon landings. After the Mercury and Gemini programs were completed, NASA began working on another program called Apollo. The Apollo spacecraft would eventually send Americans to the moon.

The space program was exciting, but it was also very dangerous. Sally and millions of other Americans realized just how dangerous the "space race" could be on January 27, 1967. That evening, three astronauts named Roger Chaffee, Gus Grissom, and Ed White climbed inside the spacecraft *Apollo 1* for a test. The test would practice the countdown and simulate a launch. Just a few minutes after the astronauts settled into the craft, Chaffee said, "I smell fire." Seconds later, the inside of the craft erupted in flames. It took six minutes for technicians to open the hatch to the craft. By then it was too late. All three astronauts were dead.

The *Apollo 1* disaster stunned the nation. Like many other Americans, Sally and her family did not think about possible tragedies. The fire made it all too clear that something could go terribly wrong. Unfortunately, the *Apollo 1* accident would not be the only time that sudden disaster would strike the space program.

NASA studied the accident in great detail. The fire had started when electrical wires short-circuited and caused sparks to ignite the nylon seats inside the craft. The craft was filled with oxygen, which is very flammable and fueled the fire. Another problem was that the hatch opened inward, which made it impossible for astronauts inside the craft to open it and escape. NASA used these findings to create a better and safer design for future *Apollo* spacecraft.

Heading East

As the space program progressed, so did Sally's academic career. In 1968, Sally graduated from the Westlake School for Girls. She was one of the top students in her class. Sally had two ambitions: She wanted to be a scientist, and she wanted to keep playing tennis. To fulfill these dreams, Sally enrolled in Swarthmore College in Swarthmore, Pennsylvania.

For the first time in her life, Sally would live away from her family. She would also be living in a part of the United States that was very different from southern California. Sally was not afraid of these challenges. She headed east, determined to succeed in her chosen fields.

3

ASTRONAUTS WANTED

Sally had no trouble handling the work at college. She entered Swarthmore as a physics major and spent hours in the laboratories and classrooms. Sally also studied the stars and planets, advancing her interest in space travel. She still loved to read and took several courses in literature.

Although she was dedicated to her classes, Sally's first love was tennis. She played in the Eastern Intercollegiate Women's Tennis Championships during her freshmen and sophomore years and won the championship both years in a row.

Coming Home

Sally was used to playing tennis all year long. However, the cold, snowy winters in Pennsylvania made this impossible, because Swarthmore had no indoor tennis courts during the years Sally attended the school. This bothered

Sally so much that she decided to leave Swarthmore halfway through her sophomore year. She transferred to Stanford University in Palo Alto, California.

Stanford is one of the best schools in the world, especially in the fields of science and math. Sally took as many courses as she could. Her classes included astronomy and astrophysics, which helped her understand the science of space.

A Love of Shakespeare

Sally also took many literature courses and ended up with a double major in physics and English literature. She said that reading literature gave her a much-needed break from the equations she faced in her other classes.

Sally's favorite courses were about the plays of William Shakespeare, the famous English author. Many students find Shakespeare's writing very complicated and hard to read and understand. However, Sally viewed Shakespeare's plays as puzzles. She later said, "I really had fun reading Shakespeare's plays and writing papers on them. . . . It's kind of like doing puzzles. You had to figure out what he was trying to say and find all the little clues inside the play to prove that you were right."

Sally's logical mind and training in the scientific method influenced her writing in English courses. She soon got a reputation for writing short, concise papers, and saw no need for the lengthy discussions that were a part of many seminars in English literature. Molly Tyson, a friend and classmate of Sally's at Stanford, admired how Sally could "always see to the heart of things. . . . Her style is to quickly think, figure it out, crystallize it."

Men on the Moon

Along with her studies, Sally remained interested in the events of the space program. The Apollo program resumed just a few months after the *Apollo 1* fire, and by the summer of 1969, nine *Apollo* craft had been tested. Astronauts on board these craft practiced each step of the moon landing. Finally, it was time for *Apollo 11* to take the final step and deliver men to the moon.

On July 20, 1969, President Kennedy's dream of landing a man on the moon came true. Millions of people around the world watched as two U.S. astronauts, Neil Armstrong and Buzz Aldrin, stepped down from the craft *Apollo 11* and became the first people to ever walk on the moon. Sally watched and cheered this incredible accomplishment. Along with the rest of the United States—and millions more around the world—Sally watched Armstrong and Aldrin walk, jump, and leap across the moon's surface in their bulky space suits. When he stepped onto the moon, Neil Armstrong had said it was "one small step for man, one giant leap for mankind." Sally agreed com-

On July 20, 1969, Neil Armstrong became the first human being to walk on the moon. This event, and the many other developments in the U.S. space program, were inspirations for Sally. (NASA Langley Research Center)

pletely with those words. She later said she would always remember where she was when Neil Armstrong became the first man to walk on the moon. She also enjoyed hearing about the scientific experiments the astronauts set up on the moon. Watching the moon landings made her even more interested in the science of outer space.

A Tough Decision

While at Stanford Sally continued to compete on the tennis courts. She was so good that some people suggested she quit school and become a professional tennis player. One of the people who suggested this was U.S. women's tennis legend Billie Jean King. King saw Sally play in a match in 1972 and recommended that Sally turn professional.

Sally thought long and hard about what King had told her. King was one of the greatest women's tennis players of all time, and her opinion meant a lot to Sally. However, Sally did not feel that she had what it took to become a professional. She did not think she could win consistently as a professional, and she refused to settle for anything less than the best. A few months after her meeting with Billie Jean King, Sally gave up the idea of playing professionally. Although she continued to enjoy tennis, she now had a new focus for her energies: science.

Still a Student

Sally graduated from Stanford in 1973 with a bachelor of science degree in physics and a bachelor of arts degree in English. She knew that she needed to continue her education in order to succeed as a scientist. So in September, she returned to Stanford to get her master's degree.

Between 1973 and 1975, Sally was part of Stanford's master of science program in physics. She specialized in astrophysics, which is the study of the physical and chemical characteristics of the stars, planets, and other parts of the universe. Sally focused on studying the X rays given off by stars.

In 1975, Sally received her master's degree in physics. However, her life as a student wasn't finished yet. She stayed at Stanford for another three years to obtain her Ph.D., or doctorate, in astrophysics. Receiving a Ph.D. is very difficult and involves a lot of hard work. As part of the program, Sally had to conduct experiments and research on a topic no one had done before. Sally remained fascinated by the X rays given off by stars. For her research project, she studied the behavior of free electrons in a magnetic field. Because she could not physically go to the stars to conduct experiments, Sally had to work with mathematical equations to show how electrons behaved and why stars gave off X rays. She also worked with lasers. These interests would later be very useful when Sally studied to be an astronaut.

Sally's studies involved more than just her research project. Like other doctoral students, she taught classes and assisted professors in the classroom. She helped them set up and conduct experiments and also helped the professors do research and write up scientific papers. Sally, who always loved research and learning new things, truly enjoyed her work.

A New Path

In 1977, Sally was almost done with her doctoral studies. It was time to think about life after school. Sally loved doing scientific research, so she decided to look for a job that involved doing research in the field of astrophysics. Like many other students, she looked at the want ads in the newspaper, hoping to find a job that sounded right for her.

One day, Sally picked up the want ads in Stanford University's newspaper, the *Stanford Daily*. One ad caught her attention. It was an ad from the National Aeronautics and Space Administration, the government agency in charge of America's space program. The ad said NASA was looking for scientists to conduct experiments on space shuttle flights. These scientists, called mission specialists, would go into space as part of a shuttle crew. Both men and women were welcome to apply.

The ad changed Sally's view of her future. Although she had been fascinated with the space program for years, she had never seriously thought about becoming an astronaut. Throughout the 1960s and 1970s, all U.S. astronauts had been men. This was partly because the first astronauts were taken from the ranks of military test pilots, who at that time were all men. The men-only rule also showed society's view of men and women at that time. Despite many accomplishments and changes in the law, women were still not considered as capable as men in fields such as science, math, or space travel.

Sally had been raised to believe that men and women were equal, and that she could do anything she wanted. Still, the idea of being an astronaut had never occurred to her. "I was interested in space but it wasn't anything I built a career around," she later told a group of young students. "Instead I planned to go into research or physics. I wouldn't have known how to prepare for a career as an astronaut even if it had occurred to me to try, since women weren't involved in the space program at that time."

Seeing the ad in the Stanford paper changed Sally's mind immediately. "Suddenly I knew that I wanted a chance to see the Earth and the stars from outer space," she later wrote. Sally wasted no time in applying for a job. She sent out her application that same day.

Tough Competition

Sally knew that getting a job as an astronaut would not be easy, and she was right. This was the first time in 10 years that NASA had hired astronauts, and many people wanted the job. More than 8,000 people answered the ad—far more candidates than NASA would ever need. More than 1,500 of the applicants were women.

NASA spent several months going over the applications. They had very strict qualifications for successful candidates. NASA was looking for people who could work as part of a team. The candidate had to be intelligent, self-confident, and logical. He or she had to remain calm under pressure and be good at solving problems and coming up with new solutions. Candidates also had to have a strong background in science or engineering, with at least three years of work experience. They had to be under 40 years old, between 60 and 74 inches tall, have good eyesight, and be in good physical condition.

Sally met all of these qualifications and had the level of academic and research experience that NASA was looking for. In October 1977, she was chosen as one of 208 finalists for the job. But she still had a long way to go before she was accepted as an astronaut.

Tests in Texas

Along with the other finalists, Sally traveled to the Johnson Space Center in Houston, Texas. Sally listened to talks about what it was like to be an astronaut. She also faced many tests at the space center. She met with psychiatrists who evaluated her mental and emotional health. Other tests asked about her background, education, interests, and work experience. Doctors evaluated her physical health. It was a tough period. Sally was usually very self-confident, but even she felt nervous after so many tests and interviews.

NASA wanted to see how the candidates responded to stressful situations. During one test, Sally had to operate a small, round compartment made of fabric. This unit was called the crystal rescue sphere. It seated only one person and was designed so an astronaut could transport another crew member to safety if no pressurized space suits were available. During this test, and other tests, Sally was monitored by medical equipment to see how her body reacted to stressful and dangerous work.

Finally, the testing was finished. Sally went back to Palo Alto to finish her schoolwork. Only time would tell if NASA would offer her a job.

"We've got a job for you"

Sally resumed her Ph.D. studies at Stanford. While she did her research and class work, she wondered if she would hear back from NASA. She really didn't think she would, and later said, "It didn't even occur to me that I'd get accepted." Finally, on January 16, 1978, Sally got the call she was waiting for.

George Abbey, a NASA official in charge of flight operations was on the phone. He told Sally, "We've got a job here for you if you are still interested." Sally was definitely interested. She immediately agreed to join the astronaut training program.

Sally had overcome amazing odds to win her position. More than 8,000 people had originally applied to be astronauts. In the end, only 35 candidates were chosen for the program. Sally was one of only six women in the program. The other five women were Anna Fisher, Shannon Lucid, Margaret Seddon, Judith Resnik, and Kathryn Sullivan. Fisher and Seddon were doctors, Lucid was a chemist, Sullivan was a geologist, and Resnik was an electrical engineer.

In 1978, NASA chose Sally to be part of its astronaut training program. (Bettmann/ Corbis)

Sally was pleased that there were other women in the class. She felt that choosing a number of female candidates showed that NASA was serious about bringing women into the astronaut program. In fact, the six new female astronauts tripled the number of female technical employees at NASA.

Before she left for NASA, Sally had one more thing to do. She had to complete her Ph.D., which she did in 1978. Now she was Dr. Sally Ride. And she was about to start a whole new adventure.

A HARD ROAD

In July 1978 Sally Ride arrived at the Johnson Space Center in Houston, Texas. She was in for a huge challenge, both physically and mentally. For Sally and the other candidates, a whole new kind of school was about to begin.

The Space Shuttle Program

The last Apollo flight was *Apollo 17,* which landed on the moon in December 1972. The Soviets never landed anyone on the moon, and the United States had clearly won the space race. However, by 1972 public interest in the moon landings had died down and many people in the government felt it was time to move on. NASA followed the moon landings with an orbiting space station called Skylab. Skylab was America's first long-term outpost in space. Astronauts spent weeks on Skylab, where they conducted experiments and discovered what it was like to live in space for more than a few days. The Soviets had space stations too and had sent up their first station in 1971. In

1975, U.S. and Soviet astronauts worked together by docking two space stations together in a project called *Apollo-Soyuz*. It was a surprising ending to a race that had once pitted the two countries against each other as bitter rivals.

By the mid 1970s, however, NASA knew it was time to move on to something new. Their goal was a reusable spacecraft that would ferry astronauts into space where they could work for a short time and then return home. The program, known as the space shuttle program, would launch astronauts into space using powerful rockets. Once the craft was in orbit, the rockets would drop into the ocean. Then the craft would return to Earth and land like an airplane. The space shuttle program aimed to make space travel routine and ongoing, unlike the moon landings, which had no real purpose after they reached their one goal. This was the program that Sally Ride joined.

ASCANs

The 35 new astronauts became a tight-knit group. They called themselves the "Thirty-Five New Guys" or TFNG, and even had T-shirts made up with TFNG printed on them. Both male and female members of TFNG trained together at the Space Center. The center had more than 17,000 employees and was set up like a college campus, with many different buildings spread out over the landscape.

Sally's official title was astronaut candidate, or ASCAN. An ASCAN's life was full of challenges. Sally spent many hours in the classroom, studying computer science, math, meteorology, astronomy, navigation, physics, and engineering. She went to many meetings and lectures on topics related to space flight. Sally also had to learn how each part of the space shuttle worked.

The Shuttle

The space shuttle has three main parts. The external fuel tank is the largest part of the shuttle. It holds the fuel burned during launch. The solid rocket boosters provide power needed to launch the shuttle and send it into orbit. The boosters and the external fuel tank disconnect and drop away from the shuttle after launch and fall back to Earth. Then they are retrieved and used for other shuttle flights.

The third and most important part of the shuttle is the orbiter. The orbiter holds up to eight crew members, along with the cargo for the trip. This was the part of the shuttle Sally and the other ASCANs had to know best. The orbiter has three levels. The top level is where the astronauts operate the shuttle controls. The mid-deck compartment provides space for eating, sleeping, and working. Most of the flight experiments are set up on the mid-deck compartment. This compartment also has an airlock that opens into the cargo bay. Finally, a third compartment below the floor holds the shuttle's operating equipment, including water pumps, electrical wiring, and air-purification systems.

Sally and the other ASCANs spent most of their time learning about the orbiter. She spent eight hours a day in a building called the Shuttle Avionics Integration Laboratory, or SAIL. SAIL was filled with

NASA's space shuttle program, for which Sally was hired, is unique in that the spacecrafts return to Earth and are reused for future expeditions. (Bettmann/Corbis)

noisy machinery. Sally worked with the SAIL crew to learn how every wire, switch, and circuit in the orbiter worked. Although she would not be primarily responsible for flying a space shuttle, she needed to know how to do the job in case another astronaut got sick or there was an emergency that forced Sally to take over the controls.

Flying High

Sally also spent about 15 hours a week in a T-38 training jet. She sat in the backseat of the jet and learned about radio communications and navigation. A second set of controls was also located in the back seat, and Sally had several chances to fly the plane herself. She enjoyed flying so much that she took extra lessons and eventually got her private pilot's license.

Survival training was another part of Sally's job. She jumped out of planes wearing a parachute that weighed 45 pounds. She jumped out of a helicopter into the water and floated on a raft for several hours. She was pushed out of a motorboat while wearing a parachute and had to take off the parachute harness quickly so she wouldn't drown.

Sally knew she had to be in top physical condition to meet the challenges of the ASCAN program. She ran four miles a day during the week, and up to 10 miles a day on weekends. She lifted weights and played tennis and volleyball.

Simulated Flight

Some of the most interesting moments of Sally's training came in shuttle simulators. Shuttle simulators help ASCANs get used to the physical difficulties of space flight by mimicking the feel of a space flight while remaining here on Earth. There are several different kinds of simulators, each focusing on a different task. The simulators include a navigation simulator, a systems engineer simulator, a shuttle training aircraft simulator, a shuttle mission simulator, and a motion base simulator. Each machine is operated by computers and other mechanical devices.

Sally spent 12 to 15 hours a week in simulators. She described the experience: "They turn you on your back and shake you and vibrate you and pump noise in, so that it's very realistic."

Astronauts experience weightlessness inside the space shuttle, so the ASCANs also needed to get used to being weightless. However, it is impossible to experience weightlessness for a long period of time on Earth, because gravity is always present. To give the ASCANs a taste of what it would be like to float in space, the candidates were taken up into a special plane called the KC-135. The KC-135 is a large transport plane, but all the equipment has been taken out of the passenger cabin, and the walls are padded. When a pilot sends the plane into a high-speed dive, the passengers experience weightlessness for up to 30 seconds. During this short time, Sally and the other ASCANs practiced eating, drinking, putting on their spacesuits, and using shuttle equipment. Perhaps the hardest thing was getting used to the nauseating effect of spinning around without gravity. So many ASCANs became sick that the KC-135 was nicknamed "the vomit comet." However, Sally managed not to throw up during this rough ride.

An RMS Expert

After a year of training, Sally officially became an astronaut in 1979. Now she was eligible to join a space shuttle crew. However, she still wasn't done studying and learning.

NASA requires that astronauts spend two to five years preparing for a unique assignment. Sally was assigned to learn how to operate the Remote Manipulator System, or RMS. The RMS is a gigantic mechanical arm used to move objects in and out of the cargo bay.

For two years, Sally did nothing but learn about the RMS. Another astronaut named John Fabian had the same assignment. Sally and Fabian traveled to Toronto, Canada, where the RMS engineers were located. Together, the astronauts studied and tested the huge mechanical arm. They worked with the RMS engineers to improve the arm's design and function. In time, Sally became so good at operating the RMS, she could do it without even thinking about it. "It got to be as natural as using tweezers on a noodle," she later said.

Other Jobs

Besides learning about the RMS, Sally had other responsibilities. She trained to be a capsule communicator, also known as a capcom. During a mission, the capcom is in direct communication with both Mission Control and the flight crew. Capcoms need to understand everything about

Sally was the first woman astronaut trained to be a capcom. Capcoms maintain direct communication between Mission Control and the shuttle crew during a mission. (NASA Headquarters—Greatest Images of NASA)

the mission and the flight procedures. They need to be able to stay calm during emergencies and convey information and instructions clearly and reliably. Sally was the first woman trained to be a capcom.

By April 1982, Sally had proven she was a capable astronaut who could handle many different responsibilities. Officials at NASA were very impressed with her, and so were other astronauts. Sally's knowledge and hard work were about to pay off.

The First Shuttle Flight

The first space shuttle had launched on April 12, 1981. The craft, named *Columbia,* blasted into orbit that morning with a crew of just two men, Commander John Young and Pilot Robert Crippen. Both men were former military pilots and had been part of the space program for many years.

Although the launch was delayed several times because of computer problems, *Columbia*'s liftoff and flight went just fine. *Columbia* spent 55 hours in space and orbited the Earth 36 times before landing perfectly on the runway of Edwards Air Force Base in the California desert. After six long years, Americans were back in space.

Mission Specialist Ride

In April 1982, NASA announced plans for its seventh shuttle mission on board the craft *Challenger*. The commander of the flight would be Captain Robert Crippen, who had already flown on the first space shuttle flight in 1981. Crippen knew that the seventh flight would be the first time the RMS would be used in space. For that reason, and because of her excellent reputation, Crippen asked Sally to be a member of his crew. Sally was happy to accept the assignment. She was so excited that when she called her parents to tell them the news, the normally calm Sally was so breathless she could hardly talk.

Along with working as a mission specialist in control of the RMS, Sally would also be the flight engineer. This job meant she would assist the commander and pilot during the most dangerous parts of the flight—ascent, reentry, and landing.

Sally was in good company as part of the *Challenger*'s crew. Along with Robert Crippen, the crew included copilot Frederick Hauck and Sally's friend and fellow mission specialist John Fabian. Later, physician and astronaut Norman Thagard was added to the crew. Thagard's job was to study the nausea that affected about half of space travelers during the first few days in space.

Media Star

Sally was the first woman to be named to a shuttle crew. She was also the youngest astronaut, since she would be 32 at the time the *Challenger* blasted off into space. These facts made Sally the center of media attention. Although she had received a lot of publicity when she was first named to the astronaut training program, that was nothing to the media demands Sally faced as part of an actual shuttle crew.

Sally was very uncomfortable with all the public attention. She had always been a private person and did not like having to talk about herself to reporters. She also worried that people would think she was chosen for the flight just because she was a woman. As she told a reporter from *Newsweek* magazine, "I did not come to NASA to make history. It's important to me that people don't think I was picked for the flight because I am a woman and it's time for NASA to send one." Sally wanted everyone to know that she had been picked for this flight solely because her abilities were needed on the trip.

George Abbey, who was now NASA's director of operations, agreed with Sally. He told reporters that Sally was chosen for the trip because of her ability to solve difficult engineering problems. He also stressed that she was a good team player who worked well with other astronauts and could put her knowledge into practice on a day-to-day basis. "Sally can get everything she knows together and bring it to bear where you need it," he said.

Commander Crippen also made it clear that Sally had been chosen because of her abilities, not her gender. He firmly told one reporter that he had never met a female astronaut who could not do the job. "We work together as a unit, but the fact that one is male and one is female, I haven't found made one bit of difference," he stated.

Sally tried her best to minimize her role as the first woman in space. She tried to make people see that she was a scientist and an astronaut who just happened to be a woman. She did not want to be treated any differently than the other crew members. However, the news media did not stop its focus on the fact that Sally was female. She constantly faced questions that had nothing to do with the important jobs she would have as a member of the crew. One reporter even asked if Sally would wear a bra during the flight!

A Match Made in Space

Sally was friendly with the other ASCANs, but she became particularly close to a candidate named Steven Hawley. Hawley was a tall, red-haired man from Kansas. He had studied to be an astronomer before joining NASA. In time, he and Sally fell in love.

Sally and Hawley were married on July 24, 1982. They were the first astronauts to marry each other. Sally flew her own plane to the wedding ceremony, which was held at Hawley's parents' house in Salinas, Kansas. The wedding was small and informal, and only Sally and her new husband's immediate families were there. The ceremony was made even more special because of the two ministers who performed the marriage. One was Hawley's father, Dr. Bernard Hawley. The other was Reverend Karen Scott, Sally's sister.

After the wedding, Sally and her husband settled into a house in Clear Lake City, Texas, near the Johnson Space Center. The couple did not have time for a honeymoon. Instead, Sally went back to work. There was still a lot to do before she could become the first woman in space.

Getting Ready

Sally and her new crewmates spent almost a year getting ready for their flight. They spent hours in the shuttle cockpit simulator and rehearsed every possible situation that might come up during a flight. They also practiced what to do in case of an emergency.

Sally and the other four crew members soon became like a close family. They shared an office at the space center and spent all their working hours together. All their hard work would pay off the following June, when the space shuttle *Challenger* finally blasted into orbit.

5

TO SPACE AND BACK

Sally Ride and the other crew members of the *Challenger* space flight trained hard for almost a year. Finally, on June 18, 1983, it was time to journey into space.

Blastoff!

The *Challenger* was waiting at the Kennedy Space Center at Cape Canaveral in Florida. Sally had to get up very early on the morning of her space flight. She donned the special blue flight suit that each of the astronauts wore. Each suit had a flag patch on the sleeve and a special *Challenger* patch on the front. She then met up with the crew for breakfast.

About three hours before the shuttle was scheduled to blast off, the astronauts rode to the launch pad in a van. Then they rode an elevator up 195 feet to the space shuttle hatch. A crowd of about 250,000 people had already

The Challenger *crew before their 1983 mission. Bottom row: Mission specialist Sally Ride, crew commander Robert Crippen, and pilot Frederick Hauck. Top row: Mission specialists John Fabian and Norman Thagard.* (Bettmann/Corbis)

gathered to watch the launch and admire the huge shuttle. Sally's family and friends were part of the crowd.

Technicians helped Sally and the others put on their helmets. Then the astronauts climbed inside the shuttle. Commander Robert Crippen and pilot Rick Hauck went in first and sat in the front. Sally and another mission specialist, John Fabian, went in next. Then Dr. Norman Thagard climbed into his spot in the mid-deck section. Once again, technicians stepped in to help the astronauts strap into their seats. Then the technicians left.

There was still an hour to go before the launch. The astronauts had plenty to do. Each one went through a list of preparations. They checked their instructions and made sure everything was safe and ready to go. Sally received a final message from her husband, Steven Hawley, who was watching from Shuttle Launch Control. "Sally, have a ball," he told her.

Finally, it was time for lift off. The clock counted down the last few seconds. Then, with a roar, the shuttle lifted up into the sky. For the next few minutes, the astronauts had a very bumpy ride. Sally later described it as "rough and loud. Our heads are rattling around inside our helmets. We can barely hear the voices from Mission Control in our headsets above the thunder of the rockets and engines." Powerful g forces pinned the astronauts back into their seats.

Suddenly, the noise and pressure ended. *Challenger* had reached its orbit around the Earth.

Flying and Floating

Once the rough conditions of the launch had passed, Sally and her crewmates could sit back and enjoy the view. The shuttle flew so fast that it circled the Earth every 90 minutes. Sally saw 16 sunrises and 16 sunsets every 24 hours.

The view from the shuttle was tremendous. The crew could see mountain ranges and canyons, deserts, and volcanoes. They could see icebergs in the oceans and even watch lightning flash in the clouds below them. Watching the changing landscapes of the Earth pass by was better than any television show Sally had ever seen. The view out of the other windows was just as good. Gazing into space, Sally could see countless pinpoints of light from stars that were closer to her than they had ever been before.

After she returned to Earth, Sally described the unique view of Earth from the shuttle. "The view of Earth is spectacular from space. Most people imagine that when astronauts look out the window of the shuttle they see the whole Earth like that big blue marble that was made famous by the flights that went to the moon. But the shuttle is much, much closer than those astronauts were. So we don't see the whole planet, the whole ball at once, we just see parts of it. But what that means is we can see a lot of detail on the surface of the Earth, so it's just a great view."

The view wasn't the only amazing thing about being in space. Sally and the other astronauts also enjoyed being weightless. Sally later described this experience as the best part of being in space. She said it was great to watch grownups turn into little kids as they enjoyed being weightless for the first time. The astronauts played a game of floating jelly beans across the cabin and catching them in their mouths. President Ronald Reagan, who was well-known for his love of jelly beans, had donated the candy to the astronauts for the trip.

Although it was fun, being weightless took some getting used to. To move from place to place, Sally had to push off from a wall. But if she pushed too hard, there was no way to slow down or stop, so she would crash into something! Eating was also complicated. The astronauts' food was dehydrated and came in small packages. The crew had to add water and sometimes heat the foods in a small oven on board the ship. The food was very sticky so it would stay on the spoons and not float away. Meals were eaten on trays that were strapped to each astronaut with Velcro, so they wouldn't float away either. If any food or drink spilled, it had to be cleaned up right away. Otherwise, crumbs and blobs of liquid would be floating around the cabin! Not only would this be messy and unsanitary, but the particles could also damage the computers and other equipment.

After Sally returned to Earth, she found that one of the most popular questions people asked was how astronauts went to the bathroom in space. The *Challenger* was equipped with a special toilet that had an air suction switch. Each astronaut had a special cone that he or she held next to the body to collect urine. To pass solid waste, astronauts strapped themselves down to the toilet seat so they wouldn't float away. The waste would then be sucked away by the air suction into a tank underneath the floor.

Washing and brushing teeth were also done a bit differently in space. Because water would float around the cabin, Sally washed her hands and face by spraying water

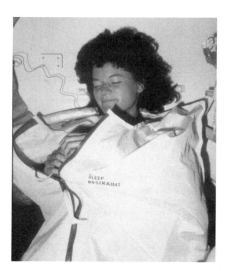

Sleeping while being weightless is just one of the practical challenges astronauts face in space. Here Sally is zipped up in a sleep restraint. (Time Life Pictures/Getty Images)

onto a washcloth, or by putting her hands into a special sealed chamber. Because water was produced as a by-product of the shuttle's fuel cells, there was plenty of water on board. When Sally brushed her teeth, she had to swallow the toothpaste and water instead of spitting it out. The astronauts did not want bits of toothpaste or water floating around the cabin!

Sleeping was also an interesting experience on

the *Challenger*. Because there was no gravity, astronauts could sleep upside-down or standing up. Sometimes they attached themselves to a wall with special sleep restraint bags, and other times they floated around the cabin. The crew also wore black eye covers so the bright sun would not wake them during the many sunrises and sunsets, and they wore earplugs to block the noises of the ship's machinery and rockets.

Getting to Work

As soon as the *Challenger* settled into its orbit, Sally and the other astronauts went to work. Each crew member had special jobs to do. One of the first jobs was to launch a Canadian communications satellite. NASA launched many satellites as a way to pay some of the enormous costs of the space program. Each satellite customer paid between $3,000 and $10,000. On this mission, the *Challenger* carried four satellites. Two would be placed in orbit, and two would be returned to Earth after testing.

Sally and John Fabian were an important part of the satellite launch. They opened the cargo bay and a special sun shield that covered the satellite. Once those steps were completed, the satellite began to spin on a turntable. When the ship was in just the right place, the *Challenger*'s computers released the satellite into orbit 22,000 miles above the Earth. A camera mounted on the satellite also took a picture of the *Challenger*. It was the first time a shuttle had been photographed in space. The next day, Sally and John released another communications satellite, this time for a customer in Indonesia.

Experiments

The astronauts were on the shuttle for six days. Besides launching satellites, Sally and her crewmates conducted scientific experiments. On board the shuttle there were 20 experiments that were prepared by high school and university students. One of these experiments studied how weightlessness affected the growth of sunflowers and radishes. Another studied the behavior of an ant colony. These experiments would help scientists understand how living things survived in the weightlessness of space, and possibly pave the way for growing foods and raising animals in space.

The astronauts were also the subject of several experiments. Every day, Dr. Norman Thagard measured their heart rates, breathing patterns, eye movements, and the pressure inside their heads. The astronauts also recorded how they felt and how being weightless affected them.

The crew documented their experience in other ways. They took photographs of each other. A television camera sent live photos back to Mission Control in Houston. The camera and the radio transmissions captured the astronauts in action. It was clear they were having a lot of fun, even while they worked hard. Sally was especially known for her jokes, and the crew often teased each other and their contacts back in Houston.

During the trip, the astronauts also looked at ways to develop new substances. Some medicines and other products are affected by weightlessness and behave differently in space. This means that some products could be manufactured in space in different or better ways than they could be made back on Earth.

The astronauts had free time on the shuttle too. They had exercise equipment, including a treadmill, because it is important to exercise to counter the negative effects weightlessness has on muscles. They also had books to read and tapes to listen to, and they could communicate with their families back home by sending radio transmissions to Mission Control.

RMS Adventures

Sally and John Fabian had spent a long time learning to work the RMS, or remote manipulator system. On the fifth day of the mission, they used the RMS to launch a satellite. This satellite was from West Germany and was called the Shuttle Pallet Satellite, or SPAS. The SPAS was loaded with 11 experiments stacked up on what looked like a flat pallet.

Sally and John worked as a team to launch the satellite. While Sally called out commands, John pushed the buttons on the control panel that moved the SPAS out of the cargo bay. Then, two hours later, John caught the satellite with the RMS and pulled it back.

Then Sally and John changed places. This time, John gave the commands and Sally operated the RMS. They released the satellite and retrieved it five times. All this happened while both vehicles were traveling through space at 17,000 miles per hour! Finally, the satellite was retrieved one last time and stored back in the cargo bay. The purpose of this project was to help astronauts learn how to catch and release satellites without using too much of the shuttle's fuel. NASA hoped to use this technique in the future to rescue damaged satellites and store them in the cargo bay, where they could be repaired and then launched back into space.

While she was working with the SPAS, Sally noticed that monitors showed the temperature of the satellite was higher when it was away from the *Challenger*. This was because there is no atmosphere in space to filter the sun's rays. Sally worried that the intense heat might damage the satellite. She suggested that the shuttle move so its shadow covered the satellite to block the direct rays of the sun. The maneuver worked, and Mission Control was pleased with Sally's quick thinking.

Home Again

June 23 was the sixth and last day of the shuttle flight. The astronauts had to get ready for landing. They put all their equipment and supplies away. They put on special pants that would increase pressure on their legs to keep their blood from pooling when the ship re-entered Earth's gravitational field. Finally, they got into their seats and prepared for landing.

During shuttle missions, Sally and the other crew members performed many experiments. (Getty Images)

The *Challenger* was supposed to land at the Kennedy Space Center at Cape Canaveral in Florida, where it had taken off six days earlier. It would be the first shuttle flight to land at the Cape, as previous flights had all landed at Edwards Air Force Base in California's Mojave Desert. However, it was raining at the Cape on the morning of the landing, and NASA officials worried that the wet weather might damage the ship's insulating tiles. These tiles cover the outside of the ship and protect it from the intense heat of re-entering the

Earth's atmosphere. NASA debated whether to extend the shuttle flight by one more day to give the weather a chance to improve. Sally and her crewmates were delighted with the idea of spending an extra day in space. Finally, however, NASA decided the shuttle would land at Edwards Air Force Base instead.

It took the *Challenger* an hour to leave its orbit, descend to Earth, and coast onto the runway at Edwards. Unlike the rocket launch of the shuttle, the ship lands like a glider. Re-entering the Earth's atmosphere and touching down on the runway was almost as turbulent and noisy as the launch had been. The *Challenger* was moving at 200 miles an hour when Robert Crippen landed it on the runway. After six days, two hours, 24 minutes, and 10 seconds and 98 orbits around the Earth, the crew of the shuttle was home, safe and sound.

Sally and her crewmates were eager to get off the shuttle and see their families and friends. But they could not just hop off and head outside. Instead, they had to get used to gravity again. After six days of weightlessness, walking and carrying heavy objects were strange to them. Sally found that even moving her hand was hard to do at first. She later said, "The crew literally could not walk down the stairs. You can stand, but you cannot walk in a straight line."

While the astronauts got used to gravity again, a crew of technicians examined the ship. They checked for any poisonous fumes, leaks, or other safety dangers. It wasn't until they were sure that everything was safe that the astronauts were allowed to leave the craft.

Because the shuttle had originally been scheduled to land in Florida, there was not a large crowd at Edwards Air Force Base to welcome the astronauts home. Still, about 125 people had gathered there. They clapped and cheered as Sally and the other astronauts walked off the shuttle. One person held a sign that read, "Herstory made today by Sally Ride." Shortly after the shuttle landed, President Ronald Reagan called to congratulate the astronauts. He told Sally, "You were the best person for the job."

The mission had gone well, and everyone was in good shape. Going into space had been a great experience for Sally. At a press conference soon after landing, she said it was the most fun she would ever have in her life.

Celebrity Sally

Sally had become a popular media star in the months after she had been chosen for the *Challenger*'s crew. But that was nothing to the attention she received when she came back from her trip.

Sally received hundreds of requests from newspapers, radio stations, and television reporters for interviews. Universities and scientific organizations invited her to speak too. Sally was overwhelmed by all the fuss. She was a private person and did not see why just doing her job should be interesting to so many people. She refused to accept invitations that did not also include the other crew members. Still, she realized that she was a role model for many people and could not avoid being singled out for special attention.

Children were especially fascinated with Sally's space flight. They had dozens of questions about day-to-day life in space, such as how the astronauts ate, showered, and went to the bathroom. Sally enjoyed talking to children and hoped she could encourage them to pursue careers in science and space exploration.

Sally spent the next year and a half making public appearances on behalf of NASA and the shuttle program. She spoke to women's groups, scientists, and government officials. She and her crewmates attended a state dinner with President Reagan at the White House and were honored when they received the keys to New York City. Sally also donated her space suit to the Smithsonian National Air and Space Museum in Washington, D.C. She even got to run in the 1984 Olympic Torch relay. She also appeared on the children's television program *Sesame Street*.

In addition to her public appearances, Sally continued to work with NASA's astronaut-training program. Because she had been in space, she could provide technicians and ASCANs with firsthand knowledge of what the astronaut experience was really like. She also had to keep up with the latest changes to the training program and study new experiments that would go up on future shuttle flights.

Back into Space

Sally dreamed of making another space flight. Her husband, Steven Hawley, finally got his chance to go into space when he was a member of the crew of the shuttle *Discovery* on August 30, 1984. Another woman from Sally's training class, Judith Resnik, was also on this flight.

On October 5, 1984, Sally's dream of returning to space came true. Once again, Sally blasted into space as a member of the *Challenger*'s crew. Once again, Robert Crippen was the commander of the journey. There were seven members of the crew this time, and Sally was not the only woman. Kathryn Sullivan, another member of her training class, would also be on board as a mission specialist. Oddly enough, Sally and Sullivan discovered that they had gone to first grade together. The other four crew members were pilot John McBride; mission specialist David Leetsma, who was an aeronautical engineer; and two payload specialists, Paul Scully-Power, an oceanographer from Australia, and Mar Garneau from Canada. This was the largest shuttle crew to date. After the flight, Sally and her crewmates would tell NASA that having so many astronauts on board made the shuttle very crowded, and they recommended that the agency not send up more than seven astronauts in the future.

Sally's first flight into space had garnered a huge amount of media and public attention. This time, however, few people seemed interested. NASA had sent up several shuttles since Sally's 1983 flight. Shuttle flights had lost their novelty, and the American public seemed to take them for granted. Another change was that it was no longer considered unusual for a woman to go into space. Women were now an accepted part of the space program. Sally was happy that this transition had happened so quickly and easily.

The October flight carried many different experiments and projects. One, called OSTA-3, featured upgraded radar instruments. Another project, MAPS, included instruments for measuring air pollution from space. FILE was an experiment to map landmarks from space.

The shuttle also carried a satellite that would collect data on the Earth's weather patterns. This data would help scientists figure out how much solar energy was reflected back into space by the Earth's atmosphere.

Problems and Solutions

Sally was in charge of releasing the weather satellite on the first day of the trip. However, she immediately ran into trouble. The hinges on the satellite's solar panels had frozen while it was in the cargo bay. To solve this problem, Sally asked Commander Crippen to reposition the shuttle so the sun could shine on the satellite and melt the ice. Sally's idea worked, and she was able to successfully launch the satellite. This was a good example of Sally's creative thinking and her ability to solve unexpected problems quickly.

Mechanical problems continued to trouble Sally and her crewmates. One of the ship's radar panels refused to close, and Sally had to use the RMS to fold it up. Other problems delayed a planned space walk for several days. However, Kathryn Sullivan and David Leetsma were able to walk in space and test a mechanism designed to help refuel satellites on future missions.

Sally and the other six astronauts landed safely at the Kennedy Space Center on October 13, after eight days in space. Despite the minor problems that had occurred on the flight, the shuttle mission went well and met all its objectives.

Back to Earth

After her return to Earth, Sally resumed her job as a NASA goodwill ambassador. She spoke to groups around the United States. She also received many honors, including the Lindbergh Eagle Award. This award was presented by Anne Morrow Lindbergh, the widow of Charles Lindbergh, who had made the first solo airplane flight across the Atlantic in 1927. The United States Department of Labor also minted two gold medallions with Sally's picture on them. Sally Ride was an American hero.

NASA continued to schedule many shuttle flights. In June 1985, Sally was chosen to make a third shuttle flight. During her training for this mission, however, a tragedy would occur that would change America's space program forever.

6

INVESTIGATING A TRAGEDY

The space shuttle *Challenger* was scheduled to go into space in January 1986. The space shuttle program had been so successful that flights had become routine. Although many Americans had lost interest in the space shuttle program, this *Challenger* flight was different. For the first time, an ordinary American—not a scientist or a pilot—would be on board.

In 1984, President Ronald Reagan announced that a teacher would join a shuttle crew. More than 11,000 teachers applied for the position. On July 19, 1985, NASA announced that Christa McAuliffe, a 36-year-old social studies teacher from Concord, New Hampshire, would be the first teacher in space.

Tragedy at the Cape

Americans followed Christa McAuliffe's training through-out 1985 and eagerly anticipated her journey into space. However, the space shuttle's launch was delayed three times because of unusually cold temperatures at Cape Canaveral. Finally, on January 28, 1986, NASA decided the launch could go ahead, even though the temperature outside was only 36° F and icicles were hanging from both the shuttle and the launch tower.

The *Challenger* blasted off with the usual roar of the engines and the billowing clouds of smoke and steam. Thousands of onlookers at the Cape and millions more watching on television cheered the launch.

For 73 seconds, everything went normally. No one noticed a small flame burst out of the solid rocket booster. Then, when the spacecraft was just 10 miles above the Earth, the *Challenger* exploded.

It took onlookers a few seconds to realize something had gone wrong. The public affairs office announcing for Mission Control could only say, "Flight controllers are looking very carefully at the situation. Obviously a major malfunction." A few seconds later, another announce-ment confirmed that the *Challenger* had exploded. Christa McAuliffe and her crewmates Francis Scobee, Michael Smith, Judith Resnik, Ellison Onizuka, Ronald McNair, and Gregory Jarvis were dead.

People all over the world were shocked and saddened by this tragedy. President Reagan had been scheduled to give his annual State of the Union speech that night. Instead, he went on television to comfort America and pay tribute to the astronauts.

The Investigation Begins

Sally Ride had been listening to the *Challenger* launch on the radio. Like other Americans, she was horrified and devastated by the tragedy. For her, the loss of the *Challenger* hit close to home. She had traveled on that ship two times. She also knew most of the astronauts who had died. Judith Resnik had been in Sally's training class and had also flown on a shuttle mission with Sally's husband, Steven Hawley.

Sally had lost friends and respected colleagues. The accident also made her realize that tragedy could strike in a second, and that an astronaut's job was indeed very dangerous.

NASA immediately launched an investigation into the tragedy. Robert Crippen was in charge of this part of the investigation, which included three planes and more than a dozen ships searching for debris over 6,000 square miles of ocean. Every piece of debris was picked up and returned to NASA, where engineers examined it for clues to what had gone so terribly wrong.

Sally Joins the Team

President Reagan wanted an independent commission to investigate the tragedy and make suggestions that would prevent a similar accident from ever happening again. The commission became known as the Rogers Commission because its leader was William Rogers, a lawyer from New York who had served as Secretary of State. Neil Arm-

Sally was part of the commission that investigated the destruction of the Challenger *in 1986, during which the crew (pictured here) was lost. From front left are astronauts Michael Smith, Francis Scobee, and Ronald McNair. Rear left are Ellison Onizuka, Christa McAuliffe, Gregory Jarvis, and Judith Resnik.*

strong, the first person to walk on the moon, was vice chair. The commission also included scientists, educators, and businesspeople. President Reagan appointed one active astronaut to the commission. That astronaut was Sally Ride.

Sally and the other members of the commission spent many, many hours studying shuttle debris and looking at photos and videotapes of the launch. They also interviewed everyone involved with the launch.

It didn't take long to figure out what had caused the explosion. A piece of rubber called an O-ring held two parts of the rocket booster together. The cold weather had caused the O-ring to crack. This allowed fire to escape from the rocket and burn through the support that held the rocket to the fuel tank. The rocket hit the fuel tank and created a terrible explosion.

Testimony revealed that engineers had tried to stop NASA from launching the *Challenger* on that frosty January morning. These engineers worried that the cold weather might cause the O-rings to crack. However, NASA was determined to launch the shuttle, especially after several days of delays. NASA's main goal seemed to have been to stay on schedule rather than worry about safety.

Sally rarely showed her emotions in public, but the information she heard at the hearings made her furious. "It's hard to stop from getting mad," she said. She realized that the tragedy could have been prevented if only NASA had been more concerned with safety and less concerned with launching the shuttle on time.

In June 1986, the Rogers Commission issued a 256-page report about the *Challenger* explosion. The report stated that NASA had serious problems with its safety procedures and engineering methods. It also revealed that astronauts were not told of any potential problems with the O-rings, and that engineers who spoke up about possible dangers were ignored. Finally, the report recommended that NASA continue to review the accident and recommended that the president order NASA to change its shuttle design and launching procedures.

A Change of Heart

Sally had been scheduled to go on her third space shuttle flight. However, after the *Challenger* disaster, NASA shut down the shuttle program for several years while it evaluated and changed its procedures.

After hearing the disturbing information presented to the Rogers Commission, Sally didn't think she wanted to go into space again. She did not feel confident or ready to take the risks.

After the Rogers Commission finished its report, NASA assigned Sally to a new job. She was now the assistant to the agency's administrator. The Rogers Commission had recommended that astronauts become part of NASA's management. This would help the space agency provide firsthand experience for its staff and for new astronauts. After all, no one knew more about a space flight than an astronaut! Sally was the first working astronaut to hold an administrative job at NASA. The new job also meant a new home. Sally was now working in Washington, D.C., rather than in Houston, Texas.

NASA had to decide the future of America's space program. The agency received many suggestions from the public, from the scientific community, and from government officials. Some people suggested NASA plan a manned mission to Mars. Others thought astronauts should go back to the moon.

As part of her administrative position, Sally wrote a report on NASA's leadership. The report was 63 pages long and was called *Leadership and America's Future in Space*. Later, the report was often called "the Ride Report" after its author. In her report, Sally looked at different options the agency could take. She wrote that she strongly believed NASA should have a broad, far-reaching purpose. It was no longer enough to send a vehicle into space, she said. Now it was time to do something important with the vehicle once it was in space.

In her report, Sally presented four major areas for NASA to focus on. The first was called Mission to Planet Earth.

This program would use information learned from space travel to study Earth. The second area was Exploration of the Solar System, including comets, asteroids, and the far reaches of the universe. Third was to create an Outpost on the Moon. Finally, NASA should work on a program called Humans to Mars, which could eventually lead to a permanent base on that planet.

Sally stressed that NASA had to keep two goals in mind as it planned future programs. First, the agency had to base everything on scientific research and technological developments. The second goal was to make sure these developments led to significant accomplishments. She wrote, "The United States will not be perceived as a leader unless it accomplishes feats which demonstrate prowess, inspire national pride, and engender international respect and a worldwide desire to associate with U.S. space activities."

Publishing Endeavors

Sally did not only write government reports. Before the *Challenger* disaster, she had been working on a book for children called *To Space and Back*. This book, co-authored by Sally's friend Susan Okie, featured dramatic, full-color photographs from Sally's space shuttle missions, as well as photographs from other space shuttle journeys. The text described what it was like to travel on the shuttle and live in space. Sally dedicated the book to her high-school science teacher, Dr. Elizabeth Mommaerts, and also to the astronauts who had been killed in the *Challenger* explosion.

NEW CHALLENGES

Sally spent 1986 and the early part of 1987 performing many different tasks. In addition to her writing and administrative duties for NASA, she continued to travel around the world, talking about the space program and her experiences. She spoke before the United Nations, encouraged young women to become scientists and astronauts, and was inducted into the National Women's Hall of Fame. Sally was a busy woman. And she was ready to change her life in a big way.

A Surprising Announcement

On May 26, 1987, Sally celebrated her 36th birthday. On that day, NASA made a special announcement. Sally was leaving NASA. She had enjoyed her years there and was pleased that the space agency's programs were now about 25 percent female—a big change from the days when Sally was one of only six women in the program! However, Sally felt it was time to move on. She planned to return to Stanford University, where she had gone to college and graduate school. Sally said, "I've always wanted to go back to a university setting. I've spent many happy years at Stanford, as a student and a graduate. I just got the right offer."

Sally provided few specific details about why she was leaving NASA. Some people thought that she was tired of working as part of management and wanted a job with more hands-on responsibilities. Others thought that she knew it was unlikely she would travel into space again. Whatever the reason, Sally felt it was time to try something new. However, 15 years later, Sally admitted in an interview that she would love to go into space again. "If they asked me . . . I'd do it in a heartbeat," she said. "On the other hand, if they asked me if I wanted to go into training for three years and then go into space again, I'd probably say no!"

NASA had only good things to say about Sally. The agency's administrator, James Fletcher, said, "The nation owes her a debt of gratitude. Her flight as the first American woman in space firmly established an equal role for women in the space exploration program. . . . The country is fortunate that her energy, intelligence, and good sense will continue to be focused on matters of vital public interest."

Sally's new job was at Stanford's Center for International Security and Arms Control. Sally would be part of the Center's special program for experienced scientists to train in matters affecting America's national security.

The year 1987 also saw a big change in Sally's personal life. She and Steven Hawley divorced. They had been married for five years and did not have any children. As usual, Sally provided few thoughts about her personal life and never publicly discussed the reason for their divorce.

New Positions

Sally remained at Stanford for two years. Then, in 1989, she accepted a job as a physics professor at the University of California in San Diego. Along with teaching, the position allowed Sally to spend a lot of time doing research. Sally had always been interested in lasers, and she now made them the focus of her research. Sally's work has helped find new uses for lasers, especially in the medical field, where they are used to make surgery quicker and safer.

Sally also served as the director of the California Space Institute until 1996. This was a research institute that was also part of the University of California's San Diego campus. Here, Sally was in charge of space-related activities. The job allowed her to pursue something that was close to her heart: encouraging young women to study science and math. As she once said in an interview, "I think it's really important that young girls that are growing up today can see that women can be astronauts too."

Through her research, Sally reached out to young women and gave them opportunities to investigate scientific careers. Sally knew that statistics showed girls and boys were equally interested in science during elementary school. However, once students reached middle school, girls' interest in science dropped drastically. She felt that this lack of interest was because girls were not encouraged to pursue science and math careers, and that the stereotype that these were "boys' activities" still existed.

Inspiring Others

Sally has always enjoyed meeting young people and encouraging them to pursue careers in science. In 1995, she and Dr. JoBea Way, a scientist at the Jet Propulsion Laboratory, created an educational program called KidSat: Mission Operations. This program was a pilot project that directly involved students at three schools with the space shuttle program. Students in the program had to plan, coordinate, and direct research projects that would travel into space on board the shuttle, which had resumed operations in 1988.

Between September 1999 and September 2000, Sally also served as President and a member of the Board of

Directors of space.com, a website about the space industry. This job helped Sally promote interest in the space program and space-related science activities to people all over the world.

Sally is especially interested in opening up the world of science to girls. In recent years, Sally has taken several steps to achieve this goal.

In September 2000, Sally left space.com to start a new project. Working with NASA, Sally founded EarthKAM, an Internet-based project that allows middle-school science classes to shoot and download photos of the Earth from space. Sally also served as the head of this project and was delighted to see its positive effect on middle-school students. The students' hands-on experience in such an awe-inspiring project was very successful in encouraging their interest in science and technology.

In 2001, Sally founded a group called Imaginary Lines. This organization supports girls who are interested in science, technology, or math. Its goal is "to increase the number of girls who are technically literate and who have the foundation they need to go on in science, math, or engineering." The organization sponsors summer camps and other programs to make science and technology fun and accessible to girls.

As part of Imaginary Lines, Sally has also founded many Sally Ride Science Clubs around the United States.

Sally is deeply involved in promoting science education for young women. Here she tells girls about a career as an astronaut at the Sally Ride Science Club's Boston Science Festival in 2002. (L. Barry Hetherington)

These clubs give girls the opportunity to work on science and math projects, consult with experts in the field, and meet other students with similar interests. Among the activities sponsored by the Sally Ride Science Clubs are a Web site, a national newsletter, science festivals, and competitions to design everything from technological toys to machines that help astronauts live in space.

Sally has also written several more children's books about the planets and other space topics. Working with co-author Tam O'Shaughnessy, she has explored such topics as Mars, the far-traveling spaceship *Voyager*, and life on Earth as viewed from space.

NASA Today

NASA has also changed its focus over the years. Space shuttle flights resumed on September 29, 1988, two years and eight months after the Challenger disaster and continued safely and routinely for many years. However, the program faced another tragedy on February 1, 2003, when the shuttle *Columbia* exploded during re-entry to Earth's atmosphere, killing all seven astronauts on board. The explosion was later traced to a piece of foam that fell off the shuttle during launch and struck heat-resistant tiles below the craft's wing. These tiles protect the craft from the intense heat that occurs when it re-enters the Earth's atmosphere. Without them, *Columbia* simply burned up.

Sally Ride was in Orlando, Florida, preparing to attend a science festival, when *Columbia* exploded. She later recalled, "We were in a hotel room watching re-entry. My first thoughts were, 'Oh, no. Not again.'" Soon after the tragedy, Sally was appointed to an independent board of experts who investigated the accident.

Sally believes that the loss of *Columbia* will not end the space shuttle program. "If you look back at the *Challenger* accident, the space program really bounced back and the program was even stronger," she told an interviewer. "I wouldn't be surprised if we see a similar thing with the *Columbia* disaster."

Indeed, NASA remains committed to the space shuttle program. The space shuttle is a key element to a bigger project—an international space station currently under construction in space. The international space station is a joint effort of several countries, including Russia (part of the former Soviet Union, which collapsed in 1991). Its goal is to serve as a home away from home in space where astronauts from all over the world can live and work together.

Many of NASA's goals are the same as the goals Sally listed in "the Ride report" she wrote in the late 1980s. NASA has sent many probes to explore the far reaches of the universe. Several spacecraft have sent back remarkable photographs of distant planets and then traveled into deep space and photographed stars, comets, and more astronomical wonders. Unmanned craft have also landed on and explored the surface of Mars, the closest planet to Earth.

A National Hero

Sally Ride remains a busy woman in the 21st century. She travels around the United States and the world, giving lectures and presentations on science, technology, and education. She continues to enjoy flying and spends much of her free time piloting her Grumman Tiger airplane. Sally also continues to teach physics and do research at the University of California in San Diego, where she concentrates on developing creative science education programs for U.S. students.

Sally has also received numerous awards for her work, both in space and on the ground. These awards include the Jefferson Award for Public Service and the Women's Research and Education Institute's American Woman Award. She is a two-time recipient of the National Space-

Sally has become a national hero as a result of her work in space, science, and education. (Getty Images)

flight Medal. One of her proudest moments was being inducted into the Astronaut Hall of Fame during a special ceremony at the Kennedy Space Center on June 21, 2003.

When she became the first U.S. woman in space in 1983, Sally Ride became a national hero. Her experiences in space have led her to believe that "Our future lies with today's kids and tomorrow's space exploration." Today, she uses her status, knowledge, and experience to encourage and teach others to reach for the stars.

TIME LINE

1951   Born on May 26 in Encino, California

1953   Sally's sister, Karen, is born

1960   The Rides spend a year traveling around Europe

1964   Receives a scholarship to Westlake School for Girls

1968   Graduates from Westlake; attends Swarthmore College in Pennsylvania

1969   Transfers to Stanford University in California

1973   Graduates from Stanford with degrees in physics and English

1975   Receives master's degree in physics from Stanford

1977   Applies for a job as an astronaut with NASA

1978   Receives Ph.D. in astrophysics from Stanford; enters NASA's astronaut training program

1982 Named to NASA seventh space shuttle mission; marries fellow astronaut Steven Hawley

1983 Becomes the first U.S. women in space on June 18

1984 Makes her second space flight

1985 Assigned to a third shuttle flight

1986 The space shuttle *Challenger* explodes shortly after launch on January 28, killing all six astronauts on board; Sally is assigned to the Rogers Commission to investigate the tragedy and make recommendations to improve NASA's safety procedures; publishes her first children's book, *To Space and Back*

1987 Publishes a report called *Leadership and America's Future in Space*; announces she is leaving NASA; accepts a position at the Center for International Security and Arms Control; divorces Steven Hawley

1988 Inducted into National Women's Hall of Fame

1989 Appointed as director of the California Space Institute; becomes professor of physics at the University of California, San Diego

1992 Publishes her second children's book, *Voyager: An Adventure to the Edge of the Solar System*

1994   Publishes her third children's book, *The Third Planet: Exploring the Earth from Space*

1995   Helps develop the KidSat: Mission Operations educational program

1996   Leaves the California Space Institute

1999   Publishes her fourth children's book, *The Mystery of Mars*; serves as President and on the Board of Directors of space.com

2000   Leaves space.com; founds and heads EarthKAM

2001   Founds Imaginary Lines

2003   Appointed to commission investigating the *Columbia* disaster; inducted into Astronaut Hall of Fame

HOW TO
BECOME AN
ASTRONAUT

THE JOB

The major role of astronauts is carrying out research; they conduct engineering, medical, and scientific experiments in space. Astronauts also operate and maintain the spacecraft that carry them and launch and recapture satellites. In the early days of space flight, spacecraft could contain only one or two astronauts. Today, a team of astronauts, each with his or her own specific duties for the flight, work aboard space shuttles and space stations.

Astronauts are part of a complex system. Throughout the flight, they remain in nearly constant contact with Mission Control and various tracking stations around the globe. Space technology experts on the ground monitor each flight closely, even checking the crew members' health via electrodes fitted to their bodies. *Flight directors* provide important information to the astronauts and help them solve any problems that arise.

The basic crew of a space shuttle is made up of at least five people: the *commander,* the *pilot,* and three *mission specialists,* all of whom are NASA astronauts. Some flights also call for a *payload specialist,* who becomes the sixth member of the crew. From time to time, other experts will be on board. Depending on the purpose of the mission, they may be engineers, technicians, physicians, or scientists such as astronomers, meteorologists, or biologists. Now that the International Space Station (ISS) has become operable, crews may vary more, as astronauts who specialize in different areas come and go from the space station on space shuttles. Up to seven astronauts at a time will be able to live and work on the space station.

The commander and the pilot of a space shuttle are both pilot astronauts who know how to fly aircraft and spacecraft. Commanders are in charge of the overall mission. They maneuver the orbiter, supervise the crew and the operation of the vehicle, and are responsible for the success and safety of the flight. Pilots help the commanders control and operate the orbiter and may help manipulate satellites by using a remote control system.

Like other crew members, they sometimes do work outside the craft or look after the payload.

Mission specialists are also trained astronauts. They work along with the commander and the pilot. Mission specialists work on specific experiments, perform tasks outside the orbiter, use remote manipulator systems to deploy payloads, and handle the many details necessary to carry out the mission. One or more payload specialists may be included on flights. A payload specialist may not be a NASA astronaut but is an expert on the cargo being carried into space.

Although much of their work is conducted in space, astronauts are involved in extensive groundwork before and during launchings. Just prior to lift-off, they go through checklists to be sure nothing has been forgotten. Computers on board the space shuttle perform the countdown automatically and send the vehicle into space. When the rocket boosters are used up and the external fuel tank becomes empty, they separate from the orbiter. Once in orbit, the astronauts take control of the craft and are able to change its position or course and maneuver into position with other vehicles.

The research role of astronauts will expand with the operation of the ISS. The station will provide the only laboratory free of gravity where scientific research can be conducted. Such an environment unmasks the basic properties of materials, and astronauts will be conducting experiments that could lead to new manufacturing processes on Earth. Scientists have high expectations for medical research that astronauts will conduct aboard the space station. It is hoped research will help fight diseases such as influenza, diabetes, and AIDS. In conducting such tests, astronauts will operate a number of special cameras, sensors, meters, and other highly technical equipment.

Another important part of an astronaut's work is the deployment of satellites. Communications satellites transmit telephone calls, television programs, educational and medical information, and emergency instructions. Other satellites are used to observe and predict weather, to chart ocean currents and tides, to measure the earth's various surfaces and check its natural resources, and for defense-related purposes. Satellites released from a shuttle can be propelled into much higher orbits than the spacecraft itself is capable of reaching, thus permitting a much wider range of observation. While on their missions, astronauts may deploy and retrieve satellites or service them. Between flights, as part of their general duties, astronauts may travel to companies that manufacture and test spacecraft components, where they talk about the spacecraft and its mission.

Astronaut training includes instruction in all aspects of space flight and consists of classroom instruction in astronomy, astrophysics, meteorology, star navigation, communications, computer theory, rocket engines and fuels, orbital mechanics, heat transfer, and space medicine. Laboratory work will include work in space flight simulators during which many of the actual characteristics of space flight are simulated along with some of the emergencies that may occur in flight. To ensure their safety while in flight, astronauts also learn to adjust to changes in air pressure and extreme heat and observe their physical and psychological reactions to these changes. They need to be prepared to respond to a variety of possible circumstances.

REQUIREMENTS
High School
High school students interested in a career as an astronaut should follow a regular college preparatory curriculum in high school but should endeavor to take as much work as possible in mathematics and science. Preparing to get into a good college is important, because NASA takes into consideration the caliber of a college program when accepting astronaut candidates. Earning the best possible score on standardized tests (ACT or SAT) will also help you get into a good college program. NASA contributes funds to 51 colleges and universities. By attending these institutions, you are ensured that the curriculum for space programs offered

will conform with NASA guidelines. To receive a list of the schools, write to: NASA Education Division, Mail Code FE, 300 E Street, SW, Washington, D.C. 20546-0001. You can also see the NASA crew-selection website at http://www.spaceflight.nasa.gov/outreach/jobsinfo/astronaut.html.

Postsecondary Training

Any adult man or woman in excellent physical condition who meets the basic qualifications can be selected to enter astronaut training, according to NASA. The basic requirements are U.S. citizenship and a minimum of a bachelor's degree in engineering, biological or physical science, or mathematics. There is no age limit, but all candidates must pass the NASA space flight physical. Beyond these basic requirements, there may be additional requirements, depending on the astronaut's role. NASA specifies further requirements for two other types of astronaut: the mission specialist and the pilot astronaut.

Mission specialists are required to have at least a bachelor's degree in one of the four areas of specialty (engineering, biological science, physical science, or mathematics), although graduate degrees are preferred. In addition, candidates must have at least three years of related work experience. Advanced degrees can take the place of part or all of the work experience requirements.

Mission specialists must pass a NASA Class II physical, which includes the following standards: 20/200 or better distance visual acuity, correctable to 20/20 in each eye, blood pressure no higher than 140/90, and height between 58.5 and 76 inches.

There are three major requirements for selection as a pilot astronaut candidate. A bachelor's degree in one of the four areas of specialty is required; an advanced degree is desirable. Candidates must also be jet pilots with at least 1,000 hours of pilot-in-command time in jet aircraft. Pilot astronauts must also pass a physical, with 20/70 or better distance visual acuity, correctable to 20/20 in each eye, blood pressure no higher than 140/90, and height between 64 and 76 inches. Because of the flight time requirement, it is rare for a pilot astronaut to come from outside the military.

Astronaut candidates undergo a year-long testing period. During this time, they are examined for how well they perform under zero-gravity conditions, in laboratory conditions, and as a member of a team with other candidates. If candidates are able to pass this first year, they are given astronaut status, and their training as astronauts begins.

Other Requirements

Astronauts must be highly trained, skilled professionals with a tremendous desire to learn about outer space and to participate in the highly dangerous exploration of it. They must have a deep curiosity with extremely fine and quick reactions. They may have to react in emergency conditions that may never before have been experienced, and to do so they must be able to remain calm and to think quickly and logically. As individuals they must be able to respond intelligently to strange and different conditions and circumstances.

EXPLORING

Students who wish to become astronauts may find it helpful to write to various organizations concerned with space flights. There are lots of books available on space exploration, both in your school and city library.

There are also several excellent websites on space exploration. NASA's website is user-friendly, with biographies of actual astronauts, advice on becoming an astronaut, and news about current NASA projects. Other interesting sites include "Ask the Space Scientist," in which astronomer Dr. Sten Odenwald answers questions at http://image.gsfc.nasa.gov/poetry/ask/askmag.html, and space image libraries with images from the Hubble Space Telescope at http://www.okstate.edu/aesp/image.html.

The National Air and Space Museum (http://www.nasm.edu) at the Smithsonian Institution in Washington, D.C., is an excellent way to learn about space exploration history. There are also several NASA-run space, research, and flight centers all over the country. Most have visitor centers and offer tours.

There are also space camps for high school students and older people all over the nation. These camps are not owned or operated by NASA, so the quality of their programs can vary greatly. Your high school counselor can help you find more information on space camps in your area.

EMPLOYERS

All active astronauts are employed by NASA, although some payload specialists may also be employed elsewhere, such as at a university or private company. All are NASA-trained and paid. Within the NASA program, astronauts may be classified as civil service employees or military personnel, depending on their background. Astronauts who gain astronaut status through their military branch remain members of that military branch and maintain their rank. Astronauts who go to college and test into the program are civil service employees.

Inactive or retired astronauts may find employment opportunities outside NASA. Jobs might include teaching at a university, conducting research for other government agencies or private companies, working with manufacturers to develop space equipment, and educating the public on the space program.

STARTING OUT

You can begin laying the groundwork toward making your astronaut application stand out from others when you are in college. Those who have been successful in becoming astronauts have distinguished themselves from the hundreds of other applicants by gaining practical experience. Internships and work/study positions in your chosen area of interest are a good way to gain vital experience. Your college placement office can help direct you to such opportunities. Working on campus as a teacher assistant or research assistant in a lab is another good way to make yourself more marketable later on.

Once other qualifications are met, a student applies to become an astronaut by requesting and filling out U.S. Government Application Form 171 from NASA, Johnson Space Center, ATTN: Astronaut Selection Office, Mail Code AHX, 2101 NASA Road 1, Houston, TX 77058. The form is reviewed at the Johnson Space Center, where all astronauts train. The application will be ranked according to height considerations, experience, and expertise. Active duty military applicants do not apply to NASA. Instead they submit applications to their respective military branch. Entrance into the profession is competitive. Aspiring astronauts compete with an average of 4,000 applicants for an average of 20 slots that open up every two years, according to NASA. From the pool of 4,000 applicants, an average of 118 are asked to come to the Johnson Space Center for a week of interviews and medical examinations and orientation. From there, the Astronaut Selection Board interviews applicants and assigns them a rating. Those ratings are passed on to a NASA administrator, who makes the final decision.

Entrance into the profession involves extensive piloting or scientific experience. Those hoping to qualify as pilot astronauts are encouraged to gain experience in all kinds of flying; they should consider military service and attempt to gain experience as a test pilot. People interested in becoming mission specialist astronauts should earn at least one advanced degree and gain experience in one or more of the accepted fields (engineering, biological or physical science, and mathematics).

ADVANCEMENT

Advancement is not a formal procedure. Astronauts who are members of the military generally rise in rank when they become astronauts and as they gain experience. Those employed by the civil service may rise from the GS-11 to the GS-13 rating. Those who gain experience as astronauts will likely work into positions of management as they retire from actual flight status. Some astronauts may direct future space programs or head space laboratories or factories. Some astronauts return to military service and may continue to rise in rank. As recognized public figures, astronauts can enter elected office and enjoy government and public speaking careers.

EARNINGS

For most, the attraction to being an astronaut is not the salary—and with good reason. The field is one of the most rewarding, but astronauts don't draw large salaries. Astronauts begin their salaries in accordance with the U.S. Government pay scale. Astronauts enter the field at a minimum classification of GS-11, which in 2004 paid a minimum of $44,136, according to the Office of Personnel Management General Schedule. As they gain experience, astronauts may advance up the classification chart to peak at GS-13, which pays between $64,035 and $83,243. Of course, there are opportunities outside NASA (although these don't involve space flight) that may pay higher salaries. Astronauts who go to work in the private sector can often find positions with universities or private space laboratories that pay six-figure salaries.

In addition, astronauts get the usual benefits, including vacations, sick leave, health insurance, retirement pensions, and bonuses for superior performance. Salaries for astronauts who are members of the armed forces consist of base pay, an allowance for housing and subsistence, and flight pay.

WORK ENVIRONMENT

Astronauts do work that is difficult, challenging, and potentially dangerous. They work closely as a team because their safety depends on their being able to rely on one another. They work a normal 40-hour week when preparing and testing for a space flight, but, as countdown approaches and activity is stepped up, they may work long hours, seven days a week. While on a mission, of course, they work as many hours as necessary to accomplish their objectives.

The training period is rigorous, and conditions in the simulators and trainers can be restrictive and uncomfortable. Exercises to produce the effect of weightlessness may cause air sickness in new trainees.

Astronauts on a space flight have to become accustomed to floating around in cramped quarters. Because of the absence of gravity, they must eat and drink either through a straw or very carefully with fork and spoon. Bathing is accomplished with a washcloth, as there are no showers in the spacecraft. Astronauts buckle and zip themselves into sleep bunks to keep from drifting around the cabin. Sleeping is generally done in shifts, which means that lights, noises, and activity are a constant factor.

During the launch and when working outside the spacecraft, astronauts wear specially designed spacesuits to protect them against the vacuum and radiation of space.

OUTLOOK

Only a very small number of people will ever be astronauts. NASA chooses its astronauts from an increasingly diverse pool of applicants. From thousands of applications all over the country, approximately 100 men and women are chosen for an intensive astronaut training program every two years. The small number of astronauts is not likely to change for the near future, and in fact, due to the *Columbia* disaster and budget cuts, is likely to decrease. Space exploration is an expensive venture for the governments that fund it, and often the program does well to maintain current funding levels. Great increases in funding, which would allow for more astronauts, are highly unlikely. While the ISS project has generated increased public interest and will likely continue to do so as discoveries are reported, the project still requires only a few astronauts at a time aboard the station.

Much of the demand will depend on the success of the space station and other programs and how quickly they develop. The satellite communications business is expected to grow as private industry becomes more involved in producing satellites for commercial use. But these projects are not likely to change significantly the employment picture for astronauts in the immediate future.

TO LEARN MORE ABOUT ASTRONAUTS

BOOKS

Aldrin, Buzz. *The Moonlandings: An Eyewitness Account.* New York: Cambridge University Press, 2002.

Kramer, Barbara. *Neil Armstrong: The First Man on the Moon.* People to Know. Berkeley Heights, N.J.: Enslow Publishers, 1997.

Reichardt, Tony. *Space Shuttle: The First 20 Years—The Astronauts' Experiences in Their Own Words.* New York: DK Publishing, 2002.

Schyffert, Bea Uusma. *The Man Who Went to the Far Side of the Moon: The Story of Apollo 11 Astronaut Michael Collins.* San Francisco: Chronicle Books, 2003.

WEBSITES AND ORGANIZATIONS

For information on space launches, the International Space Station, and other educational resources, contact

Kennedy Space Center

Visitor Complex

Mail Code: DNPS

Kennedy Space Center, FL 32899

Tel: 321-452-2121

Email: kscinfo@dncinc.com

http://www.ksc.nasa.gov

For information on aeronautical careers, internships, and student projects, contact the information center or visit NASA's website.

National Aeronautics and Space Administration (NASA)

Headquarters Information Center

Washington, DC 20546-0001

Tel: 202-358-0000

Email: info-center@hq.nasa.gov

http://www.nasa.gov

HOW TO
BECOME A
PHYSICIST

THE JOB

Physics is the most comprehensive of the natural sciences because it includes the behavior of all kinds of matter from the smallest particles to the largest galaxies.

Basic, or pure, physics is a study of the behavior of the universe and is organized into a series of related laws. Basic physics can be studied from two points of view, experimental and theoretical. A physicist may work from one or both of these points of view. The *experimental physicist* performs experiments to gather information. The results of the experiments may support or contradict existing theories or establish new ideas where no theories existed before.

The *theoretical physicist* constructs theories to explain experimental results. If the theories are to stand the test of time, they must also predict the results of future experiments. Both the experimental physicist and the theoretical physicist try to extend the limits of what is known.

Not all physicists are concerned with testing or developing new theories. *Applied physicists* develop useful devices and procedures and may hold alternative job titles. Various types of engineers, such as electrical and mechanical engineers, are trained in physics. Applied physics and engineering have led to the development of such devices as television sets, airplanes, washing machines, satellites, and elevators.

Physicists rely heavily on mathematics. Mathematical statements are more precise than statements in words alone. Moreover, the results of experiments can be accurately compared with the various theories only when mathematical techniques are used.

The various laws of physics attempt to explain the behavior of nature in a simple and general way. Even the most accepted laws of physics, however, are subject to change. Physicists continually subject the laws of physics to new tests to see if, under new conditions, they still hold true. If they do not hold true, changes must be made in the laws, or entirely new theories must be proposed.

At the beginning of the 20th century, the laws of physics were tested extensively and found to be too narrow to explain many of the new discoveries. A new body of theories was needed. The older body of laws is called classical physics; the new is called modern physics.

Classical physics is usually divided into several branches, each of which deals with a group of related phenomena. *Mechanics* is the study of forces and their effect on matter. *Hydromechanics* studies the mechanics of liquids and gases. *Optics* is the study of the behavior of light. Physicists in this field study such things as lasers, liquid crystal displays, or light-emitting diodes. *Thermodynamics* is the study of heat. *Acoustics* is the study of sound, such as in recording studio acoustics, underwater sound waves, and electroacoustical devices such as loudspeakers. The study of electricity and magnetism also forms a branch of classical physics. Research in this area includes microwave propagation, the magnetic properties of matter, and electrical devices for science and industry.

Modern physics is also broken up into various fields of study. *Atomic physics* is the study of the structure of atoms and the behavior of electrons, one of the kinds of particles that make up the atom. *Nuclear physics* is the study of the nucleus, or center, of the atom and of the forces that hold the nucleus together. *High-energy physics*, or *particle physics*, is the study of the production of subatomic particles from other particles and energy. The characteristics of these various particles are studied using particle accelerators, popularly called atom smashers.

Solid-state physics is the study of the behavior of solids, particularly crystalline solids. Cryogenic, or low-temperature, techniques are often used in research into the solid state. Research in solid-state physics has produced transistors, integrated circuits, and masers that have improved computers, radios, televisions, and navigation and guidance systems for satellites. *Plasma physics* is the study of the properties of highly ionized gases. Physicists in this field are concerned with the generation of thermonuclear power.

Although biology and geology are separate sciences in their own right, the concepts of physics can also be applied directly to them. Where this application has been made, a new series of sciences has developed. To separate them from their parent sciences, they are known by such names as *biophysics* (the physics of living things) and *geophysics* (the physics of the earth). Similarly, the sciences of chemistry and physics sometimes overlap in subject matter as well as in viewpoint and procedure, creating *physical chemistry*. In *astrophysics*, the techniques of physics are applied to astronomical observations to determine the properties of celestial objects.

Most physicists are engaged in research, and some combine their research with teaching at the university level. Some physicists are employed in industries, such as petroleum, communications, manufacturing, and medicine.

REQUIREMENTS
High School
If you are interested in becoming a physicist, take college preparatory courses. You should take as much mathematics as is offered in your school as well as explore as many of the sciences as possible. English skills are important, as you must write up your results, communicate with other scientists, and lecture on your findings. In addition, get as much experience as possible working with computers.

Postsecondary Training
Physicists may have one, two, or three degrees. Physicists at the doctoral level command the jobs with the greatest responsibility, such as jobs in basic research and development. Those at the master's level often work in manufacturing or applied research. Those with a bachelor's degree face the most competition and generally work as technicians in engineering, software development, or other scientific areas.

Some employers in industry are attracted to those with a broad scientific background. With a bachelor's degree in physics or a related science, you may be hired with the intention of being trained on the job in a specialty area. As you develop competency in the special field, you may then consider returning to graduate school to concentrate your study in this particular field.

In addition, some teaching opportunities are available to those with bachelor's degrees at the primary and secondary school level. However, in order to teach at the college level (and even at some secondary schools), you will need an advanced degree. While a master's degree may be acceptable to teach at a junior college, most universities require that professors have their doctorates. Those with a master's degree may obtain a job as an assistant in a physics department in a university while working toward a Ph.D. in physics.

More than 500 colleges and universities offer a bachelor's degree in physics, and about 250 schools offer master's and doctoral programs. The American Institute of Physics provides a list of graduate institutions; see the next chapter for contact information.

Certification or Licensing

Those who plan to teach at the secondary school level may be able to obtain a teaching position with a bachelor's degree if they also meet the certification requirements for teaching (established by the state department of education in each state). Because different states have different certification requirements, undergraduates should research the requirements for the state in which they hope to teach.

Other Requirements

Physicists are detail oriented and precise. They must have patience and perseverance and be self-motivated. Physicists should be able to work alone or on research teams.

EXPLORING

If you are interested in a job in physics, talk with your science teachers and research careers in the school library. See if your school offers science clubs, such as a physics or astronomy club, to get involved with others that hold the same interests as you. Participation in science fair projects will give you invaluable insight into theory, experimentation, and the scientific process. If your school does not sponsor science fairs, you may find fairs sponsored by your school district, state, or a science society.

EMPLOYERS

Approximately 13,000 physicists work in the United States, most of them in industry, in research and development laboratories, and in teaching. Twenty-nine percent of all physicists work for the federal government, mostly in the

Department of Defense. Other government physicists work in the Departments of Energy, Health and Human Services, and Commerce and for the National Aeronautics and Space Administration. Those working in industry jobs may hold a job title other than physicist, such as computer programmer, engineer, or systems developer.

STARTING OUT

The career services office of the college or university from which you obtain a degree will often have listings of jobs available. In addition, many industries send personnel interviewers to college campuses with physics programs to seek out and talk to students who are about to receive degrees. Students should also attend industry, career, and science fairs to find out about job openings and interview opportunities.

Those who are interested in teaching in public schools should apply to several school systems in which they may want to work. Some of the larger school systems also send personnel interviewers to campuses to talk with students who are about to receive degrees in science and who also have acquired the necessary courses in education.

Teaching jobs in universities are often obtained either through the contacts of the student's own faculty members in the degree program or through the career services office of the university.

Jobs with government agencies require individuals to first pass a civil service examination. For more information on federal employment, check out the USA Jobs website, http://www.usajobs.opm.gov.

ADVANCEMENT

High school physics teachers can advance in salary and responsibility as they acquire experience. Their advancement is also likely to be facilitated by the attaining of advanced degrees. The college or university teacher can advance from assistant to full professor and perhaps to head of the department. Higher rank also carries with it additional income and responsibilities.

The research physicist employed by a university advances by handling more responsibility for planning and conducting research programs. Salaries should also increase with experience in research over a period of years.

Physicists in federal government agencies advance in rank and salary as they gain experience. They may reach top positions in which they are asked to make decisions vital to the defense effort or to the safety and welfare of the country.

Scientists employed by industry are usually the highest paid in the profession and with experience can advance to research director positions.

EARNINGS

According to the U.S. Department of Labor, the median salary for physicists was $85,630 in 2003. The lowest paid 10 percent earned $49,880 or less; the highest 10 percent earned $131,570 or more. Physicists employed by the federal government had median earnings of $95,685 in 2003.

In 2002, median salaries for members of the American Institute of Physics ranged from $78,000 for those with a bachelor's degree to $95,000 for those with a doctorate.

As highly trained and respected scientists, physicists usually receive excellent benefits packages, including health plans, vacation and sick leave, and other benefits.

WORK ENVIRONMENT

Most physicists work a 40-hour week under pleasant circumstances. Laboratories are usually well equipped, clean, well lighted, temperature controlled, and functional. Adequate safety measures are taken when there is any sort of physical hazard involved in the work. Often, groups of scientists work together as a team so closely that their association may last over a period of many years.

Physicists who teach at the high school, college, or university level have the added benefit of the academic calendar, which gives them ample time away from teaching and meeting with students in order to pursue their own research, studies, or travel.

OUTLOOK

According to the *Occupational Outlook Handbook,* employment for physicists should grow more slowly than the average through 2012. Although increases in government research, particularly in the Departments of Defense and Energy, as well as in physics-related research in the private sector, will create more opportunities for physicists, there will be stiff competition among Ph.D. holders for basic positions. The need to replace retiring workers will account for almost all new job openings.

Private industry budgets for research and development will continue to grow, but many laboratories are expected to reduce their physics-based research to focus on product and software development and applied or manufacturing research. Opportunities will exist for physicists who work with computer technology, information technology, semiconductor technology, and other applied sciences.

Job candidates with doctoral degrees have the best outlook for finding work. Graduates with bachelor's degrees are generally underqualified for most physicist jobs. They may find better employment opportunities as engineers, technicians, or computer specialists. With a suitable background in education, they may teach physics at the high school level.

TO LEARN MORE ABOUT PHYSICISTS

BOOKS

Brallier, Jess M. *Who Was Albert Einstein?* New York: Grosset & Dunlap, 2002.

Feynman, Richard P. *Six Easy Pieces.* New York: Basic Books, 1996.

Gribbin, John R., and Mary Gribbin. *Eyewitness: Time & Space.* New York: Dorling Kindersley, 2000.

Kuhn, Karl F. *Basic Physics: A Self-Teaching Guide.* Hoboken, N.J.: Wiley, 1996.

MacLachlan, James. *Galileo Galilei: First Physicist.* Oxford Portraits in Science. New York: Oxford, 1999.

WEBSITES AND ORGANIZATIONS

For employment statistics and information on jobs and career planning, contact

American Institute of Physics
One Physics Ellipse
College Park, MD 20740-3843
Tel: 301-209-3100
Email: aipinfo@aip.org
http://www.aip.org

For information on educational requirements and careers, contact

American Physical Society
One Physics Ellipse
College Park, MD 20740-3844
http://www.aps.org

Fermilab offers internships, learning and employment opportunities, and general information about its laboratory. For more information, contact

Fermi National Accelerator Laboratory
Education Office
PO Box 500
Batavia, IL 60510-0500
Tel: 630-840-3000
http://www.fnal.gov

For career information and employment opportunities in Canada, contact

Canadian Association of Physicists

Suite 112, MacDonald Building

University of Ottawa

150 Louis Pasteur Avenue

Ottawa, ON K1N 6N5 Canada

Tel: 613-562-5614

Email: cap@physics.uottawa.ca

http://www.cap.ca

TO LEARN MORE ABOUT SALLY RIDE

BOOKS

Blacknall, Carolyn. *Sally Ride: America's First Woman in Space*. New York: Dillon Press, 1984.

Camp, Carole Ann. *Sally Ride: First American Woman in Space*. Springfield, New Jersey: Enslow Publishers Inc., 1997.

Fox, Mary Virginia. *Women Astronauts Aboard the Shuttle*. New York: Julian Messner, 1987.

Hurwitz, Jane and Sue. *Sally Ride: Shooting for the Stars*. New York: Ballantine Books, 1989.

Kramer, Barbara. *Sally Ride: A Space Biography*. Berkeley Heights, New Jersey: Enslow Publishers Inc., 1998.

Orr, Tamra. *Sally Ride*. New York: Rosen Publishing Group Inc., 2004.

Ride, Sally. *To Space and Back*. New York: Lothrop, Lee & Shepard, 1986.

Schraff, Anne. *American Heroes of Exploration and Flight.* Springfield, New Jersey: Enslow Publishers Inc., 1996.

Wade, Linda R. *Sally Ride: The Story of the First American Female in Space*. Bear, Delaware: Mitchell Lane Publishers, 2003.

WEBSITES

About Sally Ride

http://womenshistory.about.com/library/bio/blbio_ride_sally.htm

Astronaut Bio: Sally Kristen Ride

http://www.jsc.nasa.gov/Bios/htmlbios/ride-sk.html

Imaginary Lines Press Room

http://www.imaginarylinesinc.com/press/newspapers/030427KansasCityStar.shtml

Sally Kristen Ride: First American Woman in Space

http://www.lucidcafe.com/library/96may/ride.html

Sally Ride: Astronaut

http://www.enchantedlearning.com/explorers/page/r/ride.shtml

Sally Ride Science Club

http://www.sallyrideclub.com

VIDEOS

Conversations with Legendary American Women: Sally Ride. Marathon Music & Video, 1996.

Women in Space. TMW Media Group, 2000.

INDEX

Page numbers in *italics* indicate illustrations.

ABOUT THE AUTHOR

Joanne Mattern is the author of more than 125 books for children. She likes writing nonfiction because it lets her bring real people and events to life. She enjoys music, reading, baseball, animals, travel, and speaking to school and community groups about the topics in her books. She lives in New York State with her husband, three young daughters, three crazy cats, and two tree frogs.